W9-CTU-746

capricorn

december 22 • january 20

vmb
PUBLISHERS

contents

Text by
Patrizia Troni

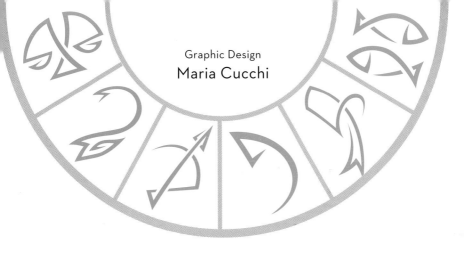

Graphic Design
Maria Cucchi

Character and Temperament

Everybody says that Capricorn has a steely character, and essentially that is correct. Capricorn is resistant, tenacious and determined; they have an exceptional iron will, they never give up; they are stubborn, and when they set themselves an objective they pursue it with all of their might until they have achieved it.

Capricorn has nerves of steel. When necessary, they can be cold, detached and impassible, not allowing themselves to be conditioned by their emotions, which they keep under rigorous control with their rationality. This latter is undoubtedly one of their qualities, which is complemented by a logical, strategic perspective that follows a precise and dependable policy and program.

Capricorn is physically strong and has a lot of stamina. They never give in to laziness or idleness, and this concrete, pragmatic and responsible attitude leads to results, which are certainly not attained through the immediacy of instinct or intuition that grasps the truth thanks to telepathic powers. No, their feet are firmly planted on the ground, they know where they began and where they want to go; they are realists who faithfully stick to the facts. But, if this were a true description of their character, we would be facing a cold, inexorable robot programmed to carry out a series of tasks, probably the most difficult ones. This is not the case.

Hidden behind their taciturn, reserved appearance, which never seems to be carried away by human weaknesses such as constant complaining or the need for protection, there is a sensitive and attentive heart that, thanks to first-class intelligence, understands that humans cannot be ruled by infantile and whiny sentimentalism, because life requires commitment and constant work.

It is perhaps due to this profound sensitivity, which avoids exaggerated displays of feeling, that already in their adolescence they realize that they cannot stand idly by and that life demands answers, answers that cannot be sought in the clouds or in vacuous fantasy or visionary idealization.

Their great determination, and capacity to view things from on high, impart orderly, lucid progression – as well as the fine qualities of measure, humility, economy and discernment – to everyday complications.

Capricorn does not get carried away or excited, they never gape like a person who comes upon something marvelous and exceptional. Their proverbial realism leads them to consider things and people exactly as they are, as they appear, without the foggy confusion and chaos of psychological projection.

Because Capricorn knows that life is difficult and entails great effort, from an early age they forge ahead. Scrupulous, intelligent and never superficial (although it would do them good to smile a bit more and give vent to spontaneous and natural feelings more often), they have a tranquil character that seeks serenity without ever relying on pipe dreams. These are qualities that often help Capricorn to attain positions of power.

Capricorn does not disdain power, because keeping everything under control is one of their distinguishing features. But, gaining power is not an egotistic or narcissistic mania; a responsible position is merely the reward for their great organizational ability.

Capricorn likes to be on high and to view the world from on high, because it is useful. From that position, they see things more clearly. This is why astrologists liken Capricorn to a wild mountain goat standing still on the tallest rock, which affords the clearest, least irritatingly entangled, and perhaps purest, view of life.

Love and Passion

8 Capricorn

Although Capricorn is a master of independence, although Capricorn is a master of self-sufficiency, dominion and control, although Capricorn likes to 'tower over' and give priority to rationality over feelings, when all is said and done this is merely appearance, because Capricorn is much more tender and gentle than at first seems to be the case.

They may be slow at falling in love and at being swept away by unbridled, sensual passion, but when their wall of mistrust and wariness is breached they prove to be lovers who are very attentive to their partner's needs, able to understand their partner deeply, to help and support their partner in making practical choices. And, when they have overcome a certain resistance and rigidity, concerning sexual desire, they are also fascinating, committed and indefatigable lovers, perhaps lacking somewhat in imagination but uninhibited and even very intense.

To be sure, they are not the type who is dominated, nor are they passive lovers who do everything their partner wants. They are not world champions of mawkish sentimentalism, fairy tale fantasy and romantic strolls under the stars. As in everything else, in love too they are essential, realistic and hardly inclined to float among the clouds of wishful thinking. But, unlike those who promise and promise, talk and

talk again, kiss and cuddle, utter endearments that may turn out to be merely empty words, they manifest their love concretely, with real substance. For them, love is not made of dreams but is a question of solid, constant, profound construction.

Capricorn does not suffocate or lean on their partner. They assume responsibility for their feelings and choices and do not depend psychologically on their partner. They are very constructive and, with time, become irreplaceable.

One can trust and depend on Capricorn. Capricorn is forthright and calls a spade a spade. And, should their partner ask for more attention, a few tender words, and perhaps more engrossing conversation, with their silence and steady but profound look they show that they are more reliable and understand the true value of love more than all the frivolous seducers in the world.

Absolute love is something that Capricorn arrives at gradually. They are not made for thunderbolts that overturn their existence overnight. With very few exceptions, decisions concerning engagement and marriage are made after a period of reflection, because Capricorn has the wisdom and rationality that allows them to evaluate every detail of the situation without being overwhelmed, like adolescents, by passing enthusiasm and feelings. People may say you are not very romantic, but this not exactly true, because real feeling does not consist only of empty words and continuous displays of affection.

While they are not the most generous people on earth – and are sometimes criticized for this – and while they are a bit cold at times and sometimes express themselves in an overly drastic tone, slowly and progressively they feel their partner become an integral part of themselves. So much so that they suffer quite a lot from separation and the pangs of love.

Their love becomes practical and highly intelligent. It is a sentiment that is often integrated into that general context of life programming that is so essential for Capricorn. What Capricorn really wants is constructive love in which their partner shares a common project, love in which both can build a solid framework of a life together.

The magic of their love reveals itself with time, and if their partner does not really share this project and proves to be destabilizing, vague, uncertain and insincere, then they go your own way, albeit very regretfully. And, in matters of love, as in everything else, once they have made a decision they never backtrack.

How to Hook a Capricorn and How to Let Them Go

At first sight, the Capricorn heart seems to be unbreachable, a safe whose combination is unknown. Capricorn is not a love-at-first-sight type, and even should attraction suddenly blaze they will never show it; for Capricorn, falling in love is not madness, but, rather, careful evaluation.

If you want to seduce a Capricorn male you must be prepared for positional warfare and not let yourself be misled by his silence or apparent coldness. He is by no means an exponent of lyrical outbursts, dreamy looks and serenades under your window. No, he is an essential, practical person for whom love does not dote on silly effusion. The fact that he is not too quick to smile does not become a torrent of passion and does not betray strong feelings must not deceive you. Behind his thick-skinned appearance is a gentle soul, a heart yearning for warmth and abandon. Although he limits his show of feeling and affection to the essential, his Capricorn heart is fragile and appreciates a caress, a gesture of tenderness or a quick kiss more than you might think. In order to win his heart you must combine massive doses of tenderness with constant, solid and sincere presence.

The female Capricorn has a strong, dominating personality. She is determined and attracted by determined men, especially those in important positions and of good social status. Lazy men, whiners or losers, men who neither act nor react, have very little chance with these women. As they are not immune to the manifestation of power, one way to conquer them is to show you have a fine automobile, classy clothes and behavior, without neglecting intense feelings. Her need for affection must be filled with tons of tenderness.

Because Capricorns invest so much in love, with their prudence and reflection, they are shattered when a relationship comes to an end. If you want to leave them, motivating all the logical steps of your choice will help them to get over this trauma.

Compatibility with Other Signs

Aries is impulsive and irrational, while Capricorn is slow and thoughtful. If we add to this the fact that both of you like to command and neither gives in easily, a relationship is possible only if the most pungent aspects of your characters are smoothed over.

With a Scorpio at their side, Capricorn will have excellent results in both the professional and financial fields. The erotic side of the relationship is also very intense, and although there are occasional clashes, overall the positive aspects outweigh the negative ones by far.

With Cancer, the physical side functions well, but the mental and practical ones will show definite signs of strain. With Taurus, Virgo and another Capricorn both will have the same rhythm, the same seriousness and the same practical and rational approach, so things couldn't be better. Capricorn loves silence and Sagittarius can't keep quiet for a second. This torrential loquacity disorientates Capricorn, but the Sagittarius energy and their confident, smiling way of establishing relationships will win Capricorn over.

Aquarius and Libra are fine for overcoming boredom and making enjoyable trips or friendships based on dialectics. Gemini transmits a good deal of verve but tends to be carefree about everything, while Capricorn takes everything seriously. Consequently, it is not easy to share the same approach to life with Gemini. Yet, different views and opinions could enhance the relationship if each of the two signs manages to understand the other's needs.

Pisces makes Capricorn fly and glide into a paradise of the senses. The Pisces extravagant behavior and delicate fragility makes Capricorn lose their head. Of course, t would like Pisces to be more conscientious, less caught up in irrational thoughts and acts. Yet the desire that flares up between them is terrific.

A relationship with Leo is just one long argument. Leo is proud and Capricorn is stubborn, and neither side will give an inch. But, in love, as in friendship, every so often there must be a compromise, a little giving way, even though Capricorn is always sure that they are in the right.

Capricorn Profession and Career

Capricorn is a tireless and dedicated worker. Of all the Zodiac signs Capricorn is perhaps the one that applies itself most, that can count on a precise, logical mind and on exhaustible physical strength.

Capricorn is serious and reliable. It is very difficult to find a Capricorn rebel, a loafer, a distracted person or one without a sense of responsibility. They are usually the first to arrive at their workplace and the last to leave. And, even when they are tired, they pretend not to notice it, perhaps because they enjoy their work and because they never leave things half finished. Watching them work, one understands why man was born as *Homo faber*, a creator or maker. Capricorn is the 'maker' of their own destiny; they do not wait for manna to fall from heaven. Whatever they achieve is rightfully earned, and the result of hard work. They make use of their great determination, commitment and stubborn constancy in order to reach a goal.

Whatever their line of work - from the most manual one of a laborer or artisan to the mental work of a clerk, manager or executive - they do their best and their performance is regular and constant. They are not

the type who go from rags to riches or vice versa, experiencing phases of incredible good luck with others of sudden collapse.

They have a marathon runner's pace, maintaining the same speed for hours without letting up. Their carburation is slow; they are diesel engine that start slowly but then never stop again.

Their body language does not betray haste, it is difficult to notice any sign of urgency in them. They do everything, arrive at everything, without being agitated because they work methodically, know how to organize themselves and are endowed with good tactics and strategy. They are great at making programs, both short- and long-term. Impulsive decision-making and impetuosity are not part of their character. They never jump in at the deep end, and even if they might have to take a risk sometimes, they make sure to examine all aspects of the potential risk before doing so.

Their superiors usually know that they are able to handle a huge workload, from both a qualitative and quantitative standpoint. And, when they are a manager they expect the same dedication and work philosophy from their subordinates, and their orders, expressed in a few words, are clear and indisputable. Their charisma affects their col-

✿   ✿   ✿   ✿   ✿   ✿   ✿

leagues with an authority that is all the more efficacious the more humble, plain and firm it is as well. Their behavior is moderate, controlled and solid.

In a way, one could say that they were born to command, that they have a natural inclination to take on the most important responsibilities. People trust them because they are serious, rigorous, enthusiastic, pertinacious and determined. They are also trusted because they demand the same quality and quantity of commitment that they demand of themselves. They are a beacon for those they work with, a rock. In the long run, they may be depended upon too much, and in this case, they will have an unreasonable workload on their shoulders.

They make for excellent entrepreneurs and professionals. They like to organize their work from beginning to end and are certainly not the type who, while caught up in their work, keep looking at their watch to see if it's time to go home.

Capricorn is particularly well suited to intellectual professions, writing, and philosophy. Many newspaper and magazine editors, heads of publishing houses, personnel superintendents, managers, printers and librarians were born under Capricorn.

How Capricorn Thinks and Reasons

Although Capricorn is often accused of having little imagination and fantasy, of being neither very quick nor exceptionally intuitive, they are among the most solid, clear-cut intellects in the Zodiac because their intellectual capacity is based on granitic logic that starts off from reality as it is and never from confused projections of their psyche. They could not do without a rational mental framework with perfectly planned coordinates. This is possible thanks to their capacity for continuous reflection, which, without too much agonizing, is always active, and under control.

While it is true that they mostly control emotions and immediate sensations, which at first they mistrust quite a lot, they slowly and progressively grasp and define data with the utmost precision and clarity, arriving at conclusions that no one will be able to dispute. The reason for this is that they may come to the point slowly, coolly and calmly, but once there, their conclusions are definitive and absolute.

Their mind is rarely agitated; on the contrary, it is usually solid and steady and can rely on a nervous system of steel that never lets itself be upset by circumstances and proceeds head-on, but always with the utmost humility. Their thinking process is connected to a pragmatic approach, so that their thoughts always have a utilitarian streak. For Capricorn, thinking is not neurotic compulsion, but an instrument for taking from reality what is useful rather than pipe dreams. Understanding is tantamount to immediate action, and abstraction as an end in itself is foreign to the Capricorn character.

They reason well because they act alone. The confirmation that they are right derives from facts; if things proceed in the right direction this means that they have understood perfectly. To their way of thinking, a table is a table and a tree is a tree, and nothing more need be said on the subject. Unlike other characters that are equally thoughtful but end up creating mental labyrinths in which they remain entangled, their clear and essential simplicity is truly precious in this respect. Without the need for ostentation, without unpleasant displays to prove that their intelligence is superior, without exhibiting the profundity of their reasoning in order to create a charismatic aura, with this simplicity they become authoritative, a point of reference for those around them who suffer from uncertainty, confusion and doubt.

Needless to say, they are not known for their mental flexibility. They are sometimes accused of being stubborn, downright obstinate and uncompromising, when they believe that their view is the correct one.

Constant and rigorous students of the world, they proceed detachedly along a straight line. Their thoughts, ideas and projects are always rational and logical and they never deviate and are never distracted or misled.

Their cold logic filters their hunches, impressions and notions, reducing them to an essential synthesis. Whatever is marginal, fancied or indefinite is immediately discarded. They are levelheaded and conscientious, and don't allow themselves to be deceived by the seduction and illusions of those who treat the mind like an object for magicians.

However, their strong and rational self should learn to loosen up, so to speak, become more elastic, and heed the voices of their spirit. Every so often, they should allow some irrationality and folly to emerge. Attach the same importance to their heart as to their head. Dreams, desires and feelings cannot always be subjected to the ironclad logic of reason.

Sociability, Communication

and Friendship

Most certainly, Capricorn prefers to be alone rather than in chaotic, too carefree and merry company. The proverb "better to be alone than in bad company" is implemented by Capricorn every day.

While this may sometimes lead them to favor their isolation, their overall behavior does not include an arrogant opposition to or detachment from social life because they feel they are not recognized for their qualities or even their greatness. Hardly any Capricorn suffers from narcissism, much less a persecution complex. If they withdraw from the world and its hustle and bustle, it is because they prefer concentration to empty and useless distraction. They dislike chaos and are not crazy about the whirlwind of sounds, colors and forms in life. Their tendency to be barely sociable should not be considered an illness but perhaps a form of wisdom.

It is other people who seek them out and who for the most part lean on them and depend on them. The contrary is rarely true, because when all is said and done they do quite well alone. This induces them to be very selective in all types of relationship. They prefer to have a few friends rather than the false friendship of the many.

True friendship is something that develops only in due time, and with time becomes stronger, profound, stable and steady. However, this does not mean that they are unable to get along in the world, quite the contrary. When their presence is requested, they are always there; but they go to parties and society events more out of a sense of duty than pleasure. In order to improve their status in the workplace they sometimes find themselves involved in circumstances in which many people are present, partly because in many cases their professional success has led to their having earned positions of responsibility.

They do not waste words in social contexts; they say only what is necessary and do so without making a mistake. But, when they must make an appearance and keep the conversation alive they succeed quite well, albeit in their deliberate, self-controlled, composed manner and with great class.

When there is a clash, or they feel they have been betrayed, in a relationship, their cold, even harsh and forbidding side emerges. In any case, in social situations their hard shell is not even scratched, they do not let themselves be overwhelmed by emotion. Their mode of communicating is lean, essential, measured; their words contain a great deal of perceptiveness and awareness; they never talk just for the pleasure of talking, but speak with logical and strategic sense, always aware of where they began and where they want to arrive. They do not embellish their talk with flowery, marvelous images, since they dislike trying to fascinate others with words. They prefer to be dry, and, at times, almost rude. They want the reality they present to others to be true and objective.

They do not like to deceive others either; if anything, they get others to express their opinion openly, inducing them to go too far, and then Capricorn uses silence as a lethal weapon. They often feel embarrassed, duty-bound to expose themselves, explain, say something and then take it back. And, all the while, they continue to listen imperturbably, impassively, but very attentively, without losing the concentration that will lead them to their conclusion – which may consist of only one word, but one of those weighty words that makes their point when it has to be made.

True, they may be somewhat unsociable, taciturn and reserved; they do not want to be liked at all costs; and to some weak souls, they may seem even bearish. But, it is equally true that in the end, without smiling too much or being uselessly light-hearted, they prove to be one of the most reliable signs in the Zodiac as far as friendship is concerned.

When Capricorn Gets Angry

Capricorn is the sign of self-control, of cold detachment from things. Capricorn is very reserved, does not like to stand out and hardly ever raises their voice. They are not much disposed toward compassion, do not tolerate weaknesses and faults, and demand the most of themselves as well as of others. This means that they can put up with a mistake, misunderstanding, or improper behavior if the other person has acted in good faith. But, this is the other's one and only chance; should it happen again they would show no pity. One can tell when they are getting angry by their look, which becomes glacial, by their authoritative tone, which admits no objections, and by their tone of voice, as sharp and as heavy as an axe.

Often, when treated unfairly they do not react immediately. First, they reflect, evaluate and analyze. If they come to the conclusion that they were in the right then they make no allowances. Their anger is cold, adamant, implacable, blind, drastic and inexorable. It is anger that has no need of shouting or demonstrative feelings to wound their 'opponent'. As silent and lethal as a ninja warrior, they go right to the heart of the matter. They are inflexible in their convictions, they defend their viewpoint obstinately (in fact, Capricorn is one of the most hardheaded Zodiac signs) and hardly ever get the worst of an argument.

Always reliable, loyal and fair, they are people of few, essential words. In fact, they cannot bear verbosity, jabberers who continue to promise but never conclude anything. Naturally parsimonious, they become angry with those who waste money, spend recklessly for superficial and superfluous things.

Capricorn is a sign of power. They are made to lead, direct, and command. When they speak, they want to be heard. If they notice a distraction, rudeness and negligence, their authoritative spirit becomes authoritarian.

Capricorn Children

A thoughtful temperament, an inclination to reflect and concentrate, are quite evident in Capricorn children. Self-control, patience and perseverance will become more and more noticeable during their growth, but, from infancy, Capricorn children distinguish themselves for their prudence, their calm and their deliberate behavior. The tendency to introversion and their reserved character must not induce one to think that they are timid and sulky, and never carefree or playful. Quite the contrary, they play with gusto, move about self-confidently and seek the company of lively play-mates. They like to be with cheerful, active and exuberant children, often becoming 'leaders' because their capacity for analysis and sensible judgment is like a bulwark for other children, a beacon in any possible storm, and their proposals and opinions are highly esteemed.

Their capacity to persevere until even the most difficult problems are solved, make them determined, attentive and scrupulous students who excel, above all, in mathematics and science. In general, they are disciplined pupils who tend not to break rules. Moreover, disobedience or trouble making on their part are hardly ever noticed, because they are the classic children who are considered models of good conduct.

If given a task, one can be sure that they will carry it out, because they are serious, responsible and diligent, and never get distracted until they have finished their job.

They like to save money and enjoy seeing their piggy bank fill up. But, they want to earn their savings; they prefer pocket money as payment earned for work they have done rather than 'gifts from heaven'.

There is a tendency to consider Capricorn children as being not very affectionate, but this is not true. Although they may not show it, they crave affection, and their parents' caresses - especially their mother's - warm their young hearts.

Music Associated

If you think that such a rational and pragmatic Zodiac sign as Capricorn can boast of no exceptional celebrities in the field of music, then you are wrong. There are two key concepts that favor musical application and study for Capricorn: the propensity for constant dedication, which is a fundamental factor in a sensitive soul, and exceptional competence. However masterful and creative musicians may be, the greatest have made their profession, be it as instrumentalists or composers, their raison d'être, not only by displaying their technical prowess, but also that strong, intense sensitivity that corresponds to the character of this Earth sign.

In any case, when considering the greats in the history of music, Capricorn cannot boast as many as other Air, Water or Fire signs. There are no truly great classical composers born under Capricorn, with the possible exception of Giacomo Puccini, who composed unforgettable operas. But, there is the great Spanish cellist and conductor

with Capricorn

Pablo Casals. In the field of light and rock music, mention must be made of the Italian Adriano Celentano, the American singer-songwriter John Denver, and three greats who helped forge the history of rock music: Rod Stewart, Syd Barrett, the brilliant and unlucky vocalist of the first Pink Floyd line-up, and above all David Bowie, who, many a Capricorn, stayed in the limelight for decades, always ingeniously alternating his 'alter egos'. Among the singers, perhaps the most representative was Donna Summer. Another great star, both for her capacity to hold the stage and the quality of her repertoire, is Annie Lennox. The greatest Capricorn musician in the history of jazz was the introverted, silent and magical trumpeter Chet Baker.

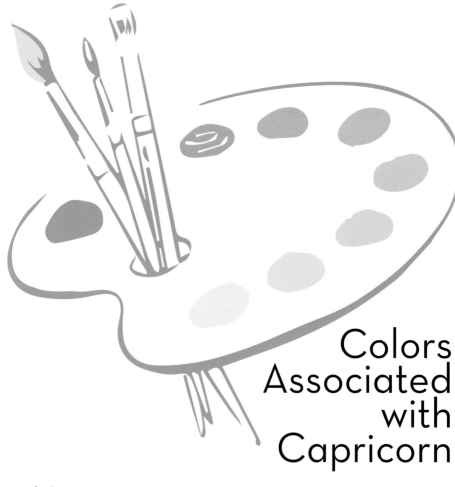

Colors
Associated
with
Capricorn

Brown, the color corresponding to Capricorn, is the hue of the patient, solid, rich and fertile earth. This color expresses the virtue of humility and poverty (monks' habits are brown), as well as strength, ferocity, power (the word 'brown' stems from the German *braun*, the color of the bear). This is color of Capricorn because, just as human labor transforms the earth, they transform, build and create their life through careful evaluation. By scrupulously measuring their steps, traveling regularly, and steering clear of dangerous deviations and distractions, they always succeed in arriving where they want to arrive. Like the earth, the color brown is concrete, stable and reliable. It is not one of the colors of the rainbow, which would seem to suggest that there is no room for reality and cold logic in dreams and unbridled fantasy. Capricorn is not a great dreamer. They might indulge in the occasional vision or chimera, but they immediately come back down to earth again. They are logical, rational, and intelligent. They never lose sight of their objectives and refuse to escape into other worlds. Brown is a warm color, and they too, under their hard protective shell, are warm, very warm. Others regard them as pillars that never collapse and on which they can lean, but while, externally, they are made of granite, their inner self is very sensitive, sweet and at moments almost fragile. When they want to isolate themselves or be sociable in tiny doses, they should wear light brown clothing – beige, sandy or camel. If, on the other hand, they want to become totally gentle and sweet and abandon their rational self-control, they should choose a warm hue of brown such as sienna. This latter is a color that stimulates friendship and acquaintances and helps them when they have to deal with important people, or those on whom they want to make a good impression. Lastly, they should choose dark brown if they must face a difficult and fatiguing task, because this hue accentuates a sense of duty and fortifies the spirit.

Flowers
and Plants
Associated
with
Capricorn

When the Sun enters Capricorn, nature stands still: snow and fog wrap everything in an unreal silence. The earth under the cold clods prepares for new life to come. Sacred to Saturn, the planet that rules Capricorn, are pine, alder and cypress trees. Touching or leaning on these trees will give Capricorn energy. Another very positive plant is mistletoe. The Druids cut it with a golden scythe the sixth night after the winter solstice. The symbol of immortality, vigor and regeneration, when placed over the front door of one's home it propitiated good luck. Pliny described it as "that which heals all", and to this day mistletoe has not lost its auspicious appeal. Other flowers connected to Capricorn are the cyclamen, clematis, nasturtium or tropaeolum, heather and chrysanthemum.

The following are the flowers and the plants for each ten-day period.

First period (December 22-31): narcissus. The emblem of vanity (in Greek mythology, the beautiful youth Narcissus who fell in love with his own reflection) as well as the eternal death-sleep-rebirth cycle, this flower favors love relationships and lends understanding and tenderness to the life of a couple. It was the fragrance of narcissus that inebriated Persephone and made her fall into the arms of Hades (the name comes from the ancient Greek word *narkào*, to daze or numb). A precious ally in seduction, the narcissus makes the beloved fall at one's feet.

Second period (January 1-10): lotus or water lily. This aquatic flower symbolizes two elements of the Capricorn nature, Earth and Water, strength and fragility. Great inner strength often leads Capricorn to protect, support and listen to others. But every once in a while they also need to rest their head on a friendly shoulder. This flower helps them to empty their mind and lighten their thoughts.

Third period (January 11-20): poinsettia (*Euphorbia pulcherrima*). With its fiery red blossom, this flower wards off all forms of melancholy and world-weariness.

Animals Associated with Capricorn

The goat is the animal-symbol of Capricorn. It is agile, frugal (it lives on very little), loves liberty and is independent, and in many ancient religions is the Mother of the world. The goat symbolizes the Capricorn ascetic, spiritual, austere side and their spirit of sacrifice (the sacrificial scapegoat). But, there is also the goat that welcomes the witches during their Sabbath, the infernal he-goat that represents the Capricorn materialistic side, which indulges in the pleasures of the senses. Like the goat, Capricorn is able to go up to the tallest peaks of compassion and altruism, but are also capable of descending into the abyss dominated by a harsh rigidity that admits of no errors. Other animals symbolically connected to Capricorn are the ibex, chamois and roe, all surefooted rock climbers, and other horned creatures such as deer, antelopes and serows. These animals symbolize an inclination to dominate, to view from on high.

The Sanskrit name for Capricorn, Makara, corresponds to the crocodile. Like this animal, Capricorn is patient and floats silently, but at the opportune moment, they launch their attack. The crocodile is also identified with the Earth-Water, matter and spirit, dualism of Capricorn.

Slow animals are also associated with Capricorn. These include the snail, the sloth and the turtle, but this does not necessarily mean that Capricorn is indolent or apathetic. It is merely a style to proceed with one's feet on the ground, inch by inch, until they reach their objective.

The jackal is also associated with Capricorn (in the Egyptian Zodiac the jackal-headed god Anubis is depicted next to Capricorn), as are the bear, the camel and the pig. Then there are the birds of Saturn, those with long necks such as the crane, ostrich and peacock, and large birds like the heron, stork and flamingo.

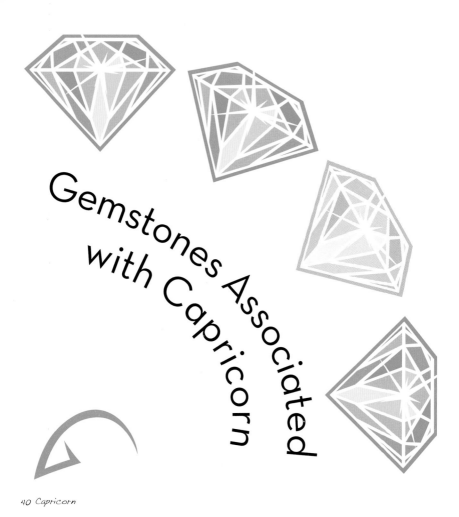

Gemstones Associated with Capricorn

The gemstones that are beneficial for Capricorn are the black opal, brown jasper and chalcedony. The opal has a wide range of nuances and colors, but Capricorn prefers the black or brown ones. This stone wards off melancholy, puts things right, reassures and amplifies all forms of consciousness. During the Renaissance, it was the symbol of purity, and people believed it imparted strength and solidity. The stone of hope, positive feelings and optimism, the opal was also known as Cupid's stone: squeeze it in your hands to charge it with desire, craving energy, and then press it to one's heart if one wants to have one's romantic desires and wishes fulfilled. The opal is particularly suitable for Capricorn because it contains water. The Water element introduces light and carefree notes in their stable, serious and conventional spirit, it sends liquid and provocative thoughts into their mind and frees them from your inner isolation. Jasper also connects Capricorn to the Water element. Some American Indian tribes called it "the water-bearing stone". The energy in jasper reduces insecurity, fear and guilt feelings; it regulates emotional earthquakes and stabilizes one's mood. It instills lunar music in the soul, proposes indolent and languid straying off course, and romantic abandon. Jasper helps to combine one's Spartan self with the power and pleasures of the heart and of the flesh.

The *Orphic Lapidary* states: "If engraved thereon is an erect Athena who is holding a bird known as a heron in her right hand and a helmet in her left hand, chalcedony will help the owner to defeat all his enemies and rivals, will render him amiable and perspicacious, able to finish everything and to overcome shipwrecks." Chalcedony helps Capricorn to avoid all forms of impasse and to face obstacles and tasks by combining a perfect spirit, lucid mind and brilliant creativity.

Best Food for Capricorn

Capricorn is not noted for being carefree and light-hearted. They have a strong ambitious side that scales the tallest peaks and another side that tends toward detachment, deprivation, and viewing life rather than living it. Capricorn is frugal, almost Spartan one could say, quite able to deny themselves everything; but they are also demanding, materialistic, and keen to enjoy and have everything. They respect life too much not to appreciate beautiful things and savor what the world offers. Their concrete and active spirit loves material life, they appreciate fine cuisine and many of them are wine connoisseurs (in fact, enology is symbolically associated with Capricorn). Capricorn includes many first-class sommeliers and great chefs. Among the various kinds of fruit, grapes and soft fruit – strongly antioxidant foods that are also rich in sugar and minerals – are Capricorn favorites. They can abandon themselves to the enjoyment of white and red grapes, gooseberries, grapes in syrup and raisins, as well as whortleberries, raspberries, blackberries and black figs. Chestnuts, a typical autumn fruit, are also well suited to Capricorn. The sea urchin that conceals its delicious pulp resembles the Capricorn spirit: seemingly intractable and closed at first sight, but very sweet if opened, if they decide to reveal themselves to others. They like to eat boiled, roasted or dried chestnuts and use chestnut flour, but do not forget to sweeten one's palate - and mood - with chestnut cream and glazed chestnuts. Saturn, the planet that rules Capricorn, is associated with the skeleton, the joints and the teeth. Useful and beneficial foods for Capricorn are those that strengthen the bones, and thus are rich in calcium and vitamin D: milk, fish, cheese, green vegetables, walnuts, beans and tofu. Among the aromatic plants, Capricorn prefers hyssop, an expectorant and digestive aid; in ancient times, it was used in purification rituals. And, to relax and help them to collect themselves, they should drink a chamomile, bearberry or valerian tisane.

Myths
Associated
with Capricorn

Pan, half-human and half goat, a powerful and wild god, is most compatible with Capricorn because he is a sylvan divinity in close contact with the earth and nature. This agile and quick-footed god moves freely through the woods, plays the flute, dances, and pursues nymphs and the pleasures of life.

Like Pan, Capricorn is a free and solitary spirit. A spirit who recharges their batteries far from crowds and civilization, always close to natural, concrete and real forces. Pan is also the symbol of carnal passion that Capricorn does not at all disregard. Indeed, Capricorn is the sign of robust desire. Capricorn may lack some fantasy in lovemaking, but is uninhibited. Potential embarrassment and prudery are very soon overcome, and when the right erotic feeling is created with their partner then they express a powerful and natural sexual desire.

The image of the goat also refers to their stubborn and determined nature, which absolutely does not take orders from others: an indomitable force that nothing and no one can move once they plant themselves squarely.

Capricorn is described as frugal, measured and parsimonious, but with a hedonistic side, a refined spirit that appreciates beautiful and costly things. Capricorn does not give in easily to uncontrolled enthusiasm and is even less likely to indulge in exhibitionism or ostentation. But, the sirens of material life certainly tempt and seduce Capricorn: new clothes, quality wine, precious antique furniture, automobiles, classy restaurants or dinners. Capricorn is capable of satisfying their every desire. This Epicurean side of the Capricorn nature connects them to Bacchus, the god of wine and the grape harvest (as we saw earlier, enology is associated with Capricorn).

On the other hand, the she-goat Amalthea, who suckled the infant Zeus, refers to the silent generosity in Capricorn. In Capricorn, egoism and rigor are combined in a surge of altruism that asks for nothing in exchange and makes others feel protected, secure and loved.

Capricorn Fairy Tale

The Snow Queen – the protagonist of the fairy tale of the same name by Hans Christian Andersen – was a very beautiful, icy, haughty woman who had become cold due to the pangs of love. Her kingdom was swept by the North Wind and was the domain of snow, cold and glacial silence. There was neither joy nor sadness or pain, because all emotions had been prohibited in her kingdom. This tale is also about a little girl and boy, Gerda and Kay, who were very close friends until a tiny piece of a shattered, evil and magical looking glass, which had the power of removing love from the human heart, went into Kay's eye, making him cruel and spiteful, which upset his friend Gerda terribly. One day the Snow Queen passed through their village. Kay was attracted by her, and the Queen had him get onto her sled, kissed him on the forehead and told him that from that moment on he would not feel the cold or sadness. Kay lost his memory and followed the Queen into her castle. Gerda, worried because she had not seen her friend for such a long time, left the village and met with many changes of fortune during her quest to find him. When she finally did, she hugged him, and her tears melted the ice in Kay's heart so that he too began to cry. In so doing, his tears caused the piece of looking glass to drop out of his eye, so that Kay became the good, dear boy he had been before, and, together, they left the icy kingdom. For Capricorn, the Snow Queen symbolizes a winter heart, the sense of solitude and isolation that they sometimes feel. They are not carefree optimists who taste life intensely and fully. They always maintain a certain aloofness, and ruthless emotional self-control. But, a caress, a friendly word, a gesture of affection, are enough to melt the ice inside them. Under their icy shell, their heart beats rapidly and is capable of great affection, friendship, and sensuality. They do not want to be moved, to succumb to mad desire, but life is pulsating inside them: thoughts fill their mind and try to melt their ironclad self-control.

PATRIZIA TRONI, trained at the school of Marco Pesatori, writes the astrology columns for Italian magazines *Marie Claire* and *Telepiù*. She has worked in the most important astrology magazines (*Astra, Sirio, Astrella, Minima Astrologica*), she has edited and written the astrology supplement of *TV Sorrisi e Canzoni* and *Chi* for years, and she is an expert not only in contemporary astrology, but also in Arab and Renaissance astrology.

Photo Credits

Archivio White Star pages 28, 34, 38; artizarus/123RF page 20 center; Cihan Demirok/123RF pages 1, 2, 3, 4, 14, 30, 48; Yvette Fain/123RF page 46; file404/123RF page 16 bottom; Olexandr Kovernik/123RF page 42; Valerii Matviienko/123RF pages 8, 12; murphy81/Shutterstock page 44; Igor Nazarenko/123RF page 40; Michalis Panagiotidis/123RF pages 20, 21; tribalium123/123RF page 16; Maria Zaynullina/123RF page 36

vmb Publishers® is a registered trademark property of De Agostini Libri S.p.A.

© 2015 De Agostini Libri S.p.A.
Via G. da Verrazano, 15 - 28100 Novara, Italy
www.whitestar.it - www.deagostini.it

Translation: Richard Pierce - Editing: Norman Gilligan

ISBN 978-88-540-2955-2
1 2 3 4 5 6   19 18 17 16 15

Printed in China